`DEC

W9-BWG-302

BUREN DISTRICT LIBRARY
CATUR. MICHIGAN 49045

DISCARDED

DEC

Fossilized!
DINOSAUR FOSSILS

By Kathleen Connors

Gareth Stevens
Publishing

12/12
grundvop

567.9
Con

Please visit our website, www.garethstevens.com. For a free color catalog of all our high-quality books, call toll free 1-800-542-2595 or fax 1-877-542-2596.

Library of Congress Cataloging-in-Publication Data

Connors, Kathleen.
Dinosaur fossils / Kathleen Connors.
    p. cm. — (Fossilized!)
Includes index.
ISBN 978-1-4339-6410-7 (pbk.)
ISBN 978-1-4339-6411-4 (6-pack)
ISBN 978-1-4339-6408-4 (lib. bdg.)
1. Reptiles, Fossil—Juvenile literature. I. Title.
QE861.5.C64 2012
567.9—dc23

                               2011018183

First Edition

Published in 2013 by
Gareth Stevens Publishing
111 East 14th Street, Suite 349
New York, NY 10003

Copyright © 2013 Gareth Stevens Publishing

Designer: Katelyn E. Reynolds
Editor: Kristen Rajczak

Photo credits: Cover, pp. 1, 5, 9, 15, 20, (cover, pp. 1, 3–24 background and graphics) Shutterstock.com; pp. 6–7 Jorg Hackemann/Shutterstock.com; p. 10 Charles Carpenter/Field Museum Library/Getty Images; p. 11 George Eastman House/ Getty Images; p. 12 SSPL/Getty Images; pp. 12–13 John Downes/Dorling Kindersley/Getty Images; p. 14 Dorling Kindersley/ Getty Images; p. 17 Ethan Miller/Getty Images; p. 19 iStockphoto.com; p. 21 Kevin Schafer/Stone/Getty Images.

All rights reserved. No part of this book may be reproduced in any form without permission in writing from the publisher, except by a reviewer.

Printed in the United States of America

CPSIA compliance information: Batch #CW12GS: For further information contact Gareth Stevens, New York, New York at 1-800-542-2595.

CONTENTS

Words in the glossary appear in **bold** type the first time they are used in the text.

THE AGE OF DINOSAURS

The first dinosaurs lived more than 200 million years ago! Most were **reptiles** that laid eggs. Dinosaurs were many shapes and sizes. The long-necked *Apatosaurus* could be more than 80 feet (24 m) long. The tiny *Hesperonychus* was smaller than a house cat!

However, dinosaurs have been **extinct** for about 65 million years. Scientists learn about them from their marks and remains, or fossils. Fossils form from plants and animals that lived thousands or millions of years ago.

THE FOSSIL RECORD

Dinosaur fossils have been found on all seven **continents**.

Many bones from the same kind of dinosaur are often found in the same place.

▽

5

SKELETAL FOSSILS

Many museums display dinosaur skeletons, or the bones that made up their bodies. However, these skeletons aren't made of dinosaurs' actual bones. They're copies of the skeletal fossils dinosaurs left behind.

Dinosaur bones turned to stone over time. The living parts of the bones broke down. This left behind the nonliving parts. Sometimes, **minerals** filled tiny open spaces in the bones. Other times, minerals entirely replaced the bone. The result was skeletal fossils. Skeletal fossils can also be claws, teeth, and other hard parts of a dinosaur.

THE FOSSIL RECORD

Many skeletal fossils formed in areas with lots of moving **sediment**, such as lakes, oceans, and riverbeds. The sediment surrounded the bones and turned into rock, which **preserved** the fossils.

Museums display copies of skeletal fossils like this *Tyrannosaurus rex* skeleton because the real fossils are very valuable.

TRACE FOSSILS

Skeletal fossils can show us what dinosaurs looked like. Trace fossils preserve facts about how they acted. **Burrows** and tooth marks are examples of trace fossils. Like skeletal fossils, these are often found in rock made from sediment.

Dinosaur tracks are some of the best-preserved trace fossils. They can tell **paleontologists** a lot about a dinosaur. Tracks can show if it was moving with a group or looking for food. From the spacing of the tracks, a paleontologist can tell if a dinosaur was walking or running.

THE FOSSIL RECORD

Tracks of many animals found together and moving in the same direction show some dinosaurs traveled in groups.

Dinosaur tracks like this one have been found in New Zealand, Mexico, the United States, and many other places.

▽

9

FIRST FINDS

In 1677, a scientist in England wrote a book that had a picture of a large bone. He thought it came from an ancient giant. It was really part of a dinosaur's thigh bone!

Around 1800, fossilized bones were found in New Jersey and in the western United States. A Connecticut man named Samuel Ellsworth Jr. found some bones while digging a well in 1818. At the time, the bones were thought to be human. However, they actually belonged to an *Anchisaurus*!

This photograph from 1894 shows scientists working with fossils.

THE FOSSIL RECORD

In 1820, Ellsworth's find was published. It's now considered the first published record of a dinosaur fossil.

This picture of a dinosaur's fossilized leg bones was taken in 1872. The man next to the bones shows how big they are.

BIG BONED

Huge fossil pieces continued to be found in southern England during the early 1800s. A scientist named Richard Owen thought the large bones came from similar, reptile-like animals. He called them "Dinosauria" in 1842.

The fossil pieces didn't show what dinosaurs looked like. In 1834, an incomplete skeleton was found near the English village of Maidstone. It was called the Maidstone *Iguanodon*, and it gave the first idea of what dinosaurs might have looked like.

Sir Richard Owen used the term *Dinosauria*, which comes from the Greek words for "terrible lizard."

The *Iguanodon* was the second dinosaur to get a name. This is its fossilized skull.

▽

THE FOSSIL RECORD

Fossil discoveries captured the public's imagination. People flocked to see full-size models at London's Great Exhibition of 1851 and other locations.

HOW OLD ARE FOSSILS?

Dinosaur fossils are different ages since dinosaurs lived on Earth for more than 160 million years. The oldest dinosaur fossils date back about 240 million years. The most recent are from about 65 million years ago, when dinosaurs died out.

How do scientists figure out how old a dinosaur fossil is? One way is to use **superposition**, which establishes the fossil's age based on which layer of rock it's in. A method called **radiometric dating** can be used to figure out the fossil's age more exactly.

As Earth ages, more rock layers form and some wear away. Many have fossils in them.

THE FOSSIL RECORD

Did you know that dinosaurs didn't disappear completely? Modern birds and crocodiles are **descendants** of dinosaurs!

Different layers of rock are easy to see in this part of Argentina.

THE DINOSAUR DIET

Fossils can tell a paleontologist what a dinosaur ate. The shape of a dinosaur's teeth tells whether they ate mostly meat or plants.

Footprints can show a dinosaur's diet, too! A footprint with three toes and sharp claws probably belonged to a meat eater called a theropod. A footprint with three rounded toes probably belonged to a plant eater called an ornithopod. A sauropod, another plant eater, had footprints of unequal sizes.

THE FOSSIL RECORD

Fossils haven't preserved the colors and patterns of dinosaurs' skin. However, some show that many dinosaurs had skin with a pebbly look.

Meat eaters had long, sharp teeth like these. Many plant eaters had flat, wide teeth.

▽

RECENT FINDS

Even though paleontologists have been uncovering dinosaur fossils for hundreds of years, there are still more to be found. In 2011, a group of scientists uncovered dinosaur fossils in Antarctica that were almost 200 million years old. They may even belong to a new **species**.

Scientists are also finding new ways to study fossils. In January 2011, Japanese scientist Tai Kubo reported he had used footprints to figure out weight. He found that flying reptiles called pterodactyls (tehr-uh-DAK-tuhlz) weighed up to 320 pounds (145 kg)!

THE FOSSIL RECORD

Only about 30 Tyrannosaurus rex skeletons have been found. Scientists think these killer dinosaurs may have been rare.

Paleontologists can spend years cleaning fossils before they start to study them.

FINDING FOSSILS TODAY

Would you like to find a dinosaur fossil? There are many places in the United States where a dinosaur fossil may be found. Paleontologists have discovered many fossils in Colorado, Montana, and Wyoming. Texas has more than 40 sites where people have found dinosaur tracks.

Many museums have dinosaur skeletons that have been put together to show the animals' size and shape. The American Museum of Natural History has a floor just for fossils. It includes two halls of dinosaur fossils.

Find fossils here!

DINOSAUR FOSSIL FACTS

- The dinosaur fossils scientists have found come from less than 0.0001 percent of all dinosaurs that lived.

- The group Richard Owen called "Dinosauria" now includes at least 1,000 species.

- Some dinosaur tracks aren't found on the ground. Over time, land shifts and moves these fossilized footprints to a canyon's wall or even a cave's ceiling.

- The first dinosaur skeleton identified in North America was a hadrosaur, or duckbill, found in New Jersey in 1858.

GLOSSARY

burrow: a hole made by an animal in which it hides or lives

continent: one of the seven large landmasses on Earth

descendant: an animal that comes from an animal of an earlier time

extinct: no longer existing

mineral: matter found in nature that is not living

paleontologist: someone who studies fossils to learn what life on Earth was like long ago

preserve: to keep safe

radiometric dating: a method of finding out how old something is

reptile: an animal covered with scales or plates that breathes air, has a backbone, and lays eggs, such as a turtle, snake, lizard, or crocodile

sediment: matter, like stones and sand, that is carried onto land or into the water by wind, water, or land movement

species: a group of animals that are all of the same kind

superposition: the placement of layers of rock on top of one another. The lower layers are older than the higher layers.

FOR MORE INFORMATION

Books

Rissman, Rebecca. *What Were Dinosaurs?* Chicago, IL: Heinemann Library, 2010.

Stewart, Melissa. *How Does a Bone Become a Fossil?* Chicago, IL: Raintree Publishers, 2010.

Websites

Dinosaur Dig
www.sdnhm.org/kids/dinosaur/
Learn more about dinosaurs and play games at the San Diego Natural History Museum's website.

Discovery Dinosaur Central
dsc.discovery.com/dinosaurs/
Read and watch videos about the latest dinosaur information.

Publisher's note to educators and parents: Our editors have carefully reviewed these websites to ensure that they are suitable for students. Many websites change frequently, however, and we cannot guarantee that a site's future contents will continue to meet our high standards of quality and educational value. Be advised that students should be closely supervised whenever they access the Internet.

INDEX